BITING MY TONGUE

BITING
MY TONGUE

Neil Astley

BLOODAXE BOOKS

ISBN: 1 85224 336 8

First published 1995 by
Bloodaxe Books Ltd,
P.O. Box 1SN,
Newcastle upon Tyne NE99 1SN.

Bloodaxe Books Ltd acknowledges
the financial assistance of Northern Arts.

Cover printing by J. Thomson Colour Printers Ltd, Glasgow.

Printed in Great Britain by
Cromwell Press Ltd, Broughton Gifford, Melksham, Wiltshire.

for Linda

Acknowledgements

Acknowledgements are due to the editors of the following publications in which some of these poems, or earlier versions of them, first appeared: *Klaonica: poems for Bosnia* (Bloodaxe Books/*The Independent*, 1993), *The Independent*, *New Statesman and Society*, *The Observer Arvon Poetry Collection* (Observer Books, 1994), *Pigeonhole*, *Poetry Review*, *Poetry Wales*, *The Printer's Devil*, *Red Herring*, *The Rialto*, *The Speechless Act* (Mandeville Press, 1984), and *The Sunday Times*.

'Manhunt' was a prizewinner in the 1993 Arvon International Poetry Competition, and was originally published as the work of Rebecca Hayes, as was 'Jasmina's House'. 'Bird Woman' was drawn from Jane Lewis's cover painting *The Magicians*, and has been set to music by George Newson. 'The Volcano' is for Anabel Gammidge, and 'The Bollocks of King Henry VIII' is for Ian Duhig (inspired by a gift). 'Paul Hill Is Doing Bird' was prompted by material left in my keeping, and is dedicated to Ken Smith. Thanks are also due to Raymond Deane and Patsy Murphy for other small thefts.

I would like to thank Northern Arts for a Tyrone Guthrie Award, and Bernard and Mary Loughlin for their warm hospitality at the Tyrone Guthrie Centre, Co. Monaghan, where many of these poems were written.

Contents

Eve's dilemma: between obedience and knowledge.
Between renunciation and appetite. Between subordination
and desire. Between security and risk. Between loyalty
and self-development. Between submission and power.
Between hunger as temptation and hunger as vision.

— GLORIA FERMAN-ORNSTEIN

The brave man carves out his own fortune,
and every man is the son of his own works.

— CERVANTES

Apocryphal

'There is no certitude outside falsification.'
ITALO CALVINO

I'm hiding out in someone else's dream,
trapped with her in the forties, in Marseille.
We're in some bonded warehouse, and I seem
to follow what the gabbling voices say

listening behind a crate die-stamped ALGIERS.
Their growling leader sounds like Jean Gabin,
his rasped argot brands them black marketeers.
Feeling something jab through my gaberdine

raincoat pocket, rubbing my leg's sore skin,
I touch a somehow familiar gun,
a Luger from the raid on Avignon,
the same cache later stolen by these men.

Hearing them yell a name which isn't mine,
it dawns on me, if they are Vichyssois
collaborators, the unknown person
who betrayed our group is a Maquisard,

a double agent. They run down the aisles
between the crates, shouting they know I'm here,
I must give myself up, but someone else
has summoned them. And then I remember

my mother's middle name, and her father
who never spoke about the Second War,
just as my gun's sent spinning through the air
and I'm overpowered, pinned to the floor,

my long hair spilling free from my man's hat.
You've got the wrong person, I say, a case
of mistaken identity. I'm not
the man whose dream this is, I'm *irlandaise*.

You are an English spy then? Gabin says,
No, I'm re-inventing myself here
through another life. I'm Rebecca Hayes
from Ireland, and you want my French gran'père,

who must have escaped, or I wouldn't be
talking to you now. Jean Gabin tests me:
What year is this then? Nineteen ninety-three.
Wrong! When were you born? Nineteen sixty-three.

Impossible! Then who is your father?
Niall Hayes, a farmer from the County Clare,
my mother's Yvette, they met here after
the war you think you're still fighting, Monsieur;

but you're a ghost now, you're only alive
in black and white rehauntings of film noirs,
celluloid dreams more real than your own life.
I like this girl, says Gabin, *she'll go far.*

Clearing the Grounds

It was three o'clock and getting dark
when father came in from the garden.
He ran the cold tap over his hands,
the water frothing to communion wine.

I turned away when he said over
the rushing of that strawberry water:
Don't you want to know the worst?
How many there were? I shook my head.

I'll tell you anyway. There were twenty
in the shed, and I slew each one with my spade.
I found the first-born huddled by the old pond
and despatched them with just a little splashing.

The women were easy. I held their heads
and gave them one bullet each, a kneeling job,
back of the neck. They all complied.
I followed my instructions to the letter.

Hunched over the stainless steel sink, he made
a hawking noise, and pranged it with his spit,
like a tin-can rattled with a practice shot.
His back huge as a crow's, his body stiffened.

When he turned to me, I knew he'd want
to beat my backside with the gleaming spade.
He had that wild look in his eyes,
like a priest who is sure of his ground.

Master says obey, but I'll stand up
on my hind legs, though I sway like a drunk.
If I can't slip this leash, I'll see his eyes
bulging like a dog's, my jaw clamped round
his jerking arm: the fingers I once licked

I'll bite off, crunching knucklebones to taste
forbidden flesh beneath his salty skin.
I want to know the Moor. What held me back,
call it habit or the easy life, was
nothing to wilderness. I could have played

his pet, become the old retainer sprawled
across the hearth. But fire's in my eyes,
by torchlight they're red as coals. My mouth
glows sulphur-yellow, tongue lolling ahead
divining water, testing air for food.

I'm hungry but have kicked away the bowl
branded with his name for me. I'm hungry
as hell, for his damnation, not bondage
from tins, not meat the price of his abuse;
hungry to hunt down what I need, snatch it

on the hoof, hungry as the loyal poor
asking for change. I want another life.
He makes his answer with a gun: five shots
ring out in the dark, one grazes my ear.
He can't shoot straight. He's shaking like a leaf.

Closer, Master. Let me lick you again.
When I was a pup, he came to me at night.
He put it on my tongue. My clumsy teeth
flecked blood in drools of dangling cuckoo-spit.
One bullet left. *You feeling lucky, Master?*

Manhunt

Months it took to find him, stalking our prey
at gatherings of squawking friends: someone
standing quietly, who didn't belong,
a stranger at a party, a new face
in the busy pub, someone on the edge
whom no one really knew, and wouldn't miss.

Some I followed home, watching how they moved
around their territory, checking their hours,
their tastes and habits. Others I tracked down
office corridors, to name-plates on doors,
telephone voices heard in rooms; I brushed
past them in the lift, offering a smile.

I tried out chance encounters in the street,
searching for the right face, the eager look
that showed intelligence, the body borne
with easy confidence, a hint of good.
None was what we wanted: all had that faint
quiver betraying pride, those tell-tale lips.

Then a gentle voice heard across a room
when I wasn't listening: I saw him caught
in sunlight by a window, a forest
of people standing between; like a doe
grazing in a clearing, he must have sensed
me there, meeting my eyes as I moved in.

Flooding the ceiling, moonlight made a pool
I floated from that night, a mirror where
I saw him moving on me, his bare back
and white globes of buttocks, his mane my hands
were raking. Out of my body, high as
a hawk, I watched my quarry wait for me

to fall down like a spider on its thread.
We lay there heavy in each other's arms,
and when he felt me breathing evenly,
he slipped away. The night he disappeared
it was as if I'd eaten him alive,
he'd gone completely. You were there instead.

Jasmina's House

We count the seconds after the thunder
till smoke puffs up and blackbirds scatter
down the valley. From there the track rises
to our crossroads, where the way divides:

north to the white town, next the top road
haunted by irregulars from either side, then
the other snaking to the pass through rock
St Sava milked to feed his wolf militiamen,

its limestone crumbling to dust with the bones
and tattered clothes of fleeing villagers.
Armoured dragons terrify the crossroads;
grinding up the hill, they swivel sharply,

stare right through our doorless broken house,
our windows emptier than eye sockets,
to where those blackbirds rise like gunsmoke
or damnation over the outer suburbs of hell.

This room was Adnan's, whose skull wobbles
below like a bleached and bearded turnip
in the gully rubble, a flutter of peonies
pleading around him, red as bullet-holes.

I remember how our butcher Ensud
wagged a finger to drive home a point,
snatching it back to tip his scales.
We paid dearly for our meat.

Ensud knifed my brother too, and cousin Budo,
but left my mother for Milanovic
who used to sell her milk. They tipped
her body down the well, then came for me.

My ransacked room is silent but for mice
tearing at my hairbrush for their nests
(they'll need my hair when winter comes).
As blood hardens on the wooden floor

my body's shape is leaving the bed,
rain easing it back into a mattress slab.
A cold wind rustles through my school papers,
the diary splayed open where it fell,

pages blurring into blackness as the ink
spreads, marking my life at the front,
leaving blank the lost white months
of empty time, from June to December.

The Volcano

I warned her not to go up there alone.
They never listen. 'But I want to see
the volcano, it may be smoking but
my guidebook says it isn't dangerous.'

The volcano, no; the mountain though is
not what it seems, that white smoke spiralling
like steam from a kettle, those paths which lead
to strange dead ends above the precipice.

'It says there hasn't been a lava flow
since 1932.' I know, I saw
that one, my father grabbed me from my bed:
'The sleeping dragon is awake,' he said.

I saw its red eyes firing all the trees,
its coal-fire hulk spilling like a bee swarm
down the valley, where it stopped at the edge
of the village. It was ten years before

they let us back, those whose homes had not
been sectioned off into the army zone.
You see beyond that barbed-wire fence, dark soil
richer than ours? That belonged to Gomez,

his family's land since my grandfather's day.
He could have grown peach trees if he'd come back,
they had a fine house too, that white ruin
you see exposed there like a broken tooth.

The woman? Yes, she'd the usual backpack,
enough food for two nights, she said, in case
the darkness caught her or the clouds came down.
English I'd say, polite, not loud and gauche

like the others, those American girls,
but wouldn't wait for help. I don't blame her
for that, some guided groups have not come back.
There was that other lava flow last year

the papers weren't allowed to mention
because of the restrictions. That envoy
from the Consulate, we met his questions
with blank stares, warned beforehand by the priests.

Father Xavier's the one to beware, goes
to meet the Governor. That torn soutane,
too black for a man of God, a bat's wing,
brown marks like burns along its ragged hem.

He has a high voice, likes to talk about
our Holy Father's greatest sacrifice,
giving up his only Son that we poor
sinners might live. They say the Governor likes

his conversation. Not me, he gives me
the jitters, that bird-voiced priest. Soldiers keep
their distance too when he's around, you'd think
he was some kind of dignitary. I made

the error, once, not thinking he could hear,
repeating my grandmother's story, how
as a girl she'd seen the mountain cave where
the dragon slept. 'She was an evil witch,

your granny,' Xavier squeaked, 'you villagers
like your superstitious tales, you peasants
know nothing.' That's right, our sharp Jesuit
returned just yesterday, another trip

to see his friend the Governor. He went
straight to the barracks. If you want to speak
with him, don't say who told you, please, he thinks
I'm a crazy old hag, he'd prefer me

safe in the grave. But don't go yet, he gives
the soldiers absolution at this hour.
Our windows will be shuttered when we hear
his black Mercedes on the empty road.

The Road

The road was always out there, a white thread
across the valley, a scar she exposed
pulling back the blinds at daybreak. It drew
his eye, like a wound or missing limb, towards

the woods where cars emerged as far-off shapes
murmuring like wind through ancient water-pipes,
a low drone rising to the burning roar
of their old gas-range, as he watched them

move along the line of levée and field,
making for the island. At night the glow
of headlights and the distant hum
were comforting, as he felt her warm arms,

her steady breathing, hold him while they slept.
East was the city, from where, when war came,
the limping cars of refugees stumbled
along the road, their lights dimmed. In the dark

he listened for their wheezing, an engine's
cough like a poorly child, the heightened pitch
of a wrong approach, a gearbox wrenching
at the bend; he searched the night like an owl

tuned to a higher frequency, his ears
expecting some disturbance, a scrabbling fox
at the wire, the worry of a lone plane
circling near, the uncertainty of cars

heading west. Months later, with some alarm,
they woke to a stuttering like small arms
from the island, then the road rumbling.
Dawn showed a line of trucks and APCs,

the grey troops of the government forces;
they saw a red Republican fighter
come in low to strafe the column, shockwaves
shaking all their windows. Yet both sides stayed

away from them, no one approached the house;
they watched the frontline as they worked the land,
a filmshow seen while stooped to milk the cows.
When silence came, they hoped to hear the cars,

but the road stayed motionless, overgrown
like a disused airstrip. It disappeared,
a skein of mist dispersed by morning sun,
a childhood memory she vaguely recalled

as he moved across her belly like rain
shadowing their fields, his tongue's trail glistening
on her milky stretchmarks. She drew him down
that way, where tawny hairs were growing wild.

Goodbye to All That

Your wayward eyes have followed me
from Rome. You broke the bank that night,
you hit a lucky streak. But then
in Prague your silver tongue cost me
my place at the Conservatoire:
how could you think I'd let it slither back?
No more this lying between us.

Where did you learn your arrogance?
The Officers' Academy
where your dressage was admired?
You call me buckish but I'm not
your filly now; this pretty mare
will please itself, won't turn at your command.
No more this lying between us.

Your rapier cuts me worse than words,
cold steel across my lover's bed.
I wouldn't be seen dead with you:
that tickly beard I used to kiss
would be a barbed wire brush against
my skin, coarser than your cavalry twill.
No more this lying between us.

How can you know me when you mock
the Pankhursts, when you scorn my love
because he's working for the Webbs?
How could you think I would betray
their trust for one last night with you?
Your time has gone. You've joined the other side.
No more this lying between us.

You're wanted by your regiment.
No matter that you won't return,
you have no right to be here now.
I will not hold you till you've gone
or kiss you till your lips are cold:
I only want you as a memory.
No more this lying between us.

You're charging off to battle blind,
tilting at tanks and mortar shells.
You know a shrapnel mat will not
protect your blinkered mount, you're past
helping her now. By dawn she'll lie
with you, deceived by automatic fire.
No more this lying between us.

The past is dying with the ghosts
I comfort in the hospital.
If any part of you survives
I'll know you when they bring you in,
I'll see the starlight in your eyes
flickering out from twenty years ago.
No more this lying between us.

I'll pull the sheet up when you fall
asleep... and drift across the night's
black mudscapes like a creeping mist,
a yellow dew of mustard gas
dissolving into air. Your blood
will make these into poppy fields.
No more this lying between us.

Now the war has ended, I lay
to rest what's left of you. Alive,
I feel your kisses, shocked at how
they reach me from another time:
all those white crosses on the hill
like ox-eye daisies with their yellow heads.
No more this lying between us.

The Smallest Hair

I test the hair-trigger, halt as my will
falters: he wants to feel the tip between
his lips, the slightest pressure now would blow

his pretty face away. He's urging me
to let him have a single, sudden burst
as his release; a feather touch to kill,

a fingertip. Don't stop, his frightened stare
and lovely mouth demand, his fearful look
like some poor creature in a snare. The gun

lowered, my arms hang down as if I've shot
my load, although I'm stock-still as a hare,
still hesitating as his frantic eyes

accuse me like a lover I've betrayed.
Above the battlefield, a buzzard keens
over the singing of artillery.

This wanting me to kill him's killing me.
I couldn't harm the smallest hair of him.
His soul is pulling to break free, to brave

the smoke-puffs powdering the heavens, like
the red balloon the kid hares after in
that film. He dies, the boy with his balloon.

The Big Sea

Her skin had a salty taste when she leaked
from the navel. She lay back on the bed,
her body clammy from the plastic sheet
stretched beneath her like a boat's tarpaulin,
growing more waterlogged as the tide rose

lapping at the crusted groynes of her legs
where sodden hair streamed out into seaweed.
Her head bobbed from side to side, her mouth
a fountain spouting fish she tried to land
in a blue-rimmed kidney dish, to let us

check them for signs of sea-lice or fin-rot.
We fussed round her like tugs when a sprat flopped
down her cheek, trying to regain her mouth.
Now the tangle of brown bladderwrack's thick
inside her: the more we pull out, the more

it thrives like a tapeworm, leaving her sore
each time she passes water. Her lungs are
sponges we can't clean out with pumps and tubes
acting as overflows. The sea's become
unstoppable, pouring out from every

opening it finds. We paddle round the bed,
ankle-deep in the sand-bagged room. I hold
her hand as the water reaches our knees.
She stares out from her pillow with a look
that says *Don't let me drown.* We mop her brow

for forty days until the level falls.
She spits her last fish out, a mackerel, as
I'm scrubbing slime from slippery floor-tiles:
I never liked fish. A turtle dove flies
down, cooing through a beak of cotton wool.

Wasted

She's growing thinner, the flesh is almost
dropping off her now. She doesn't fight him
when he comes home at midnight, eight-pints
roaring drunk from the Duke of Transylvania.

He watches a late horror flick, calls her *woman*
when he hits her, when he wants his fry-up
of bacon and black pudding, *bleeding woman*
when he shakes her awake, when he climbs

on top and judders to his quick relief.
He feigns disgust when her hair comes out
as he pulls her head to him, to suck at
those same holes, returning to favourite wounds

like a jackal worrying a carcass
he's come upon, which something else has killed;
drops her when bored after gorging his fill,
wandering off for his washbasin ritual.

With that red gash of a mouth, he becomes
an ageing tart, lipstick daubed on like war paint;
cupping his hands, he sluices clean his smile,
brushes those spiky teeth till they sparkle.

She hears him on the toilet, then descending
the stairs to the cellar, with his usual
parting shot of *Wake me when it's evening*.
She checks the coffin when she cannot sleep,

assures herself with the feel of the lid,
the thrum of him dozing in the warm fug,
the methane blasting of another fart.
His mind is out communing with the Powers,

playing the overnight markets with a vengeance;
he's merging his shadow companies, making
a killing with a Fluid Exchange Rate.
In this other life he's Mister Darkness,

master of the night network, refugee
turned money-man, a demon with his cash
injections, his liquid assets held back
or disappearing. She knows about his late

withdrawals, eleventh-hour switches,
how the slaughter of Black Friday happened
at his bidding; and how he's screwing her
for all she's worth. The crack-lined mirror

on her wall reflects her broken looks,
the pieces she has left. It calls her Failure
of Nerve, and Absence of Recovery,
tells her she's staring defeat in the face,

that Drac in the Box will win her over
to his side, his cloak a black manifesto
lined red with lies. Dabbing her neck
with cotton wool, the white fluffiness

soggy with witch-hazel, she watches
the redness spreading like a culture dish:
it seeps like one of his six new diseases,
like his latest virus, the one he picked up

cheap at the National Exhibition Centre,
brought home and gave her like a child.
She tried a razor then, but he thrilled her wrists,
dragged her gasping back from the newly dead.

She tried escape but his task force scoured
the city, found her floating in its lifeblood.
She tried a wooden stake but couldn't find
a heart to pierce. Her silver crucifix

he took and rammed inside her just for kicks,
urged on by cheering members and their guests
he took inside her head, to view her dreams,
the Chief Commissioner holding her down

while the heads of British industry rolled
about in ecstasy. The inspectors agreed
she might suffer some discomfort, but
she must believe the cuts he had to make

were for her own good, a necessary
sacrifice, a safe way of protecting
his investments while she's bottoming out.
Despite special bleeding, they gave her

a clean bill of health, though she knows her flesh
is falling like the value of the pound,
her falling dream a downward spiral
she cannot break while he's plugged into her,

while zombies from the execution squad
of the Blood Bank of Iran are draining
their blasphemers to death, pumping them dry,
a million barrels a day, enough for all

the bird-brained martyrs of their Holy War,
camping up their deadly Revolution in Taste.
The Black Count is a cable subscriber,
his coffin link-up draws his dividend

and funds his Cutting Edge of Fashion Show.
Now he makes her tread the catwalk like a wraith.
She's Queen of the New Look, her waif-like
body the essence of our Nouveau Poor,

her tight waist and flat breasts are *in* this year,
her skin beaten to an airy thinness.
The Count beams like a boy as she shows off
his new collection to buyers and press.

With her dark and haunted eyes, she's daring
the frantic men shooting off their Leicas;
with her brazen stare, she's a refugee
dying before their pictures reach the screen.

When a rat in a dinner-jacket gnaws her
with rag-trade talk, how well she looks
in her tatters, the oily Count moves in.
And no one sees that he's taking her out,

wasting her, feasting off the bare patches
of flesh his clothes expose, her neck flushed red
beneath his choker; as her own blood comes
in her mouth, she feels the faintness she fears

pulling her down, the pain catching her throat.
And no one wants to know how she's been beaten
within an inch of her life. Her life not his
or theirs to waste. Her wasted, wasted life.

The Miners' Wives Picket the Beardmore Glacier

We saw further than anyone knew was
possible; this our one comfort, the miles
and miles of sky-blue ice and ice-blue sky,
a minty froth of snow dancing off the mountains

out into the iceblink over glacier
and picket line, snow in the far distance,
tingly snow you felt you could almost taste
yet in a world as far away as home,

somewhere beyond the cold in which we swayed
like lumbering reptiles in our padded gear,
each movement an ache, slowing down like fish
in water freezing to a block of ice.

Day 50 of the Strike, and our noses
and cheeks were raw with frostbite; my lips
cracked, I'd lost all sense of taste, our oatmeal,
pemmican and biscuits blander than nothing.

We plundered coal for camp-fires, heating ice
not for water you could drink in sips
but Fluid Intake gulped back like a town
swallowing a flood, or a flood a town.

It felt like that, something big the women
all defied, which kept us there, something big
we all believed in, bigger than the Strike
we'd taken on to shame the men, bigger than

the whole continent of Antarctica.
It quashed the squabbling over rations,
the petty jealousies we put behind us,
the bickering in the tent we ridiculed

as *bollocking*, what we women didn't do.
Boredom was a test of will as much as cold,
the men had all walked out into the snow
but we'd resisted, heroic, holding out.

No giving in, no going back
however ill we felt, however sick of snow:
Divide by six and stay united,
six into six is one we chanted

to the hiss of the sled through ice, or trudging
against headwinds through powdery snow
that had looked so easy, above howling cross-
winds, and the Ski-doo engines' endless noise.

The police were waiting on the glacier,
a row of shields glinting along the ridge
in an icy smile of tombstone teeth
like an advert for AIDS or Steradent.

Black gauntleted, dapper in white polar gear
they banged the ground, an icy chattering
eerie in empty Antarctic air. They
clattered down the slope, swinging baseball bats

like propellors, until we rose as one
above them, six Gore-Texed women puffed up
like airships, six Angels of Redemption
swooping down on them with tins of beef,

felling the once cocky now *oh-so-surprised*
South Atlantic Constabulary,
their crack élite riot squad panicking
like gulls as bully beef hit skull and brain

to the airborne call of *Six into Six*,
Ice Is Nice and *South Pole Not North Dole.*
As they scattered, dropping clubs and shields,
shedding their uniforms, we saw they weren't

policemen but a team of husky dogs,
army conscripts drafted from the Arctic.
We passed a husky corporal yelping
for dear life, left him yapping, left other

whining stragglers as the wind took over,
trying to beat us back, our bouncing sleds
hurtling out of control. We weren't prepared
for Summer Camp, for the disappointment,

finding they'd reached the Base ahead of us.
Slumped on the ice, the Abomination
lay face down, clubbed to the ground like a seal,
her grey suit sprinkled in a shroud of snow,

a knife like a clockwork key in her back,
a red rosette of blood frozen like her smile
where her own dogs had turned on her.
We tried to find her conscience, but the savage

wind had taken what was left; a three-day
whiteout blizzard blanking out all traces
of the colour blue, from sky (now white),
from sea (reflecting sky), from quilted parkas,

from hoods and helmets of the dog police
(now pink with polka dots or frilly white).
And when the wind died down, we watched
the constables in starched-white petticoats

glide across the silky ice like ballerinas,
pulling the sledded Abominable
with frozen grin, bedecked with several kinds
of fish, herring, mullet, sad-eyed mackerel,

flown in from England by the RAF
for her funeral in the Patriot Hills.
An army penguin raised its orange beak
to sound *The Last Post*, as a Falklands sheep

intoned a poem by Tennyson (*Ulysses*,
'to strive, to seek, to find and not to yield'),
tossing a few sprats as they winched her down
an ice crevasse deeper than a lift-shaft,

her grinning face and all those beady fish-eyes
disappearing into white and greyness,
greyer than the eager, restless greyhounds
sniffing the privates, the murky greyness

of the piss-stained ice walls and washed-out sky,
the dismal grey of England in the fifties
filling all Antarctica with greyness
like poverty, the greyness of cheating

and diplomacy. The wind was whispering
around me like Iago, hissing words
it had picked up eighty years ago
from noble Captain Scott: *This is an awful place,*

and terrible enough to have laboured to it
without the reward of priority.
The wind sounded pleased with itself.
It whooped around us. It bit us hard.

East of Easter

For years they came in wonder, filing past
his waxy russet-bearded face. Kazakhs
and Tadjiks saw their colossus, tall as
the Caucasus. Uzbeks and Oyruts gazed
on living legend, the titan who shook

the earth, whose speech made land and landlords quake.
His right hand held the sun, his left a beam
of moonlight flooding the mausoleum.
Awe-struck Ostyaks came from the north to look
at the hunter who'd slain their enemies

on the ice, clubbed the fur-traders like seals,
gave their blood-money and dogs to the poor.
Kirgiz men said Redbeard could overpower
the evil one, drive him beneath the seas
with his magic ring, and knowing no night,

he never slept, withered kulaks with light
from his glowing eyes. He rode a white horse
to lift Armenia's yoke, and stirred up wars
on an eagle's back, putting Whites to flight
from the air; stood atop an armoured car

fist raised at the Finland station, called for
action, with Trotsky now invisible
seen at his side by Petrograd people
welcoming the sealed train, when Commissar
Stalin ran to kiss his turned cheek, a sign

he was his dear disciple (the Georgian
plotting behind his back). When he suffered
heart arrest, he let himself be martyred,
tied with tubes to his deathbed like Aslan,
but breathing into a thousand statues

lifted up his stone-like fist in cities
all over Russia, held out for the day
he'd rise again, when medalled dwarfs would try
to pull him from plinth with ropes and pulleys,
bind him like Gulliver trussed on a truck,

parade him prone through the streets of Simbirsk.
Toy soldiers jerked to life then as he'd proph-
esied, switched off his life support, shut off
the flow of visitors. When the clockwork
generals came to the bed where he'd lain in

state since '24 they found not the man
but a shadow stain like the Turin shroud.
He melted like a wraith into a crowd
of waiting statues moving in a line
like androids, trailing rope and scaffolding.

Vladimir Ilyich in the van, standing
fist raised like an icon, marched his statues
out of Moscow. Where the Volga elbows
the Don, a thousand giants turned, stepping
the steppes like nightwalkers. So Lenin led

his lumbering host out of the promised land,
through the Aral seabed to Samarkand
where Uzbeks joined the horde. On they headed
east of Easter, till he rose: his red beard
caught the light, sun spoke of the dawn ahead.

Blackened Blues

A body bag unzipped itself
and slipped a no good body loose.
It toasted its own blackened health,
fired off a tirade of abuse,
death cries, its blackened body blues:

'Let cockerels crow the firestorm glow
when missiles cruise your streets at night.
Let heads and tails spin round with rounds
of red and yellow tracer light.
Death dances to the blackened blues.'

'When gunships home in on your homes
a crowded shelter's your best bet:
its infra red is easy meat
for a heat-seeking exocet.
Death cries your blackened body blues.'

'The curfew wakes at crack of dawn
when guns are chattering like cold teeth.
Let bullets sing out in the trees.
The convoy sighs without relief.
Death dances to the blackened blues.'

'Nowhere to run on a death march
when mortars pound the town ahead.
Children are slow. They're first to go
when snipers earn a pound a head.
Death cries their blackened body blues.'

'My fighters are all irregulars,
their semtex breath's like marzipan.
The safe areas are never safe
except to death's militiaman.
Death dances to the blackened blues.'

'The clampdown brings on a seizure,
the ceasefire holds in its breath.
The bread queue's panned with hot crossfire.
The unmarked van delivers death,
death cries, those blackened body blues.'

The Fist

At first there was just the fist, locked away
until some drunken hothead smashed its cage
and let it fly about; as tempers flared,
it shook itself and strutted round the room,

crashing on the table, demanding that
we show it some respect. After the fight,
we bundled it off like an awkward guest.
It clenched itself, nursed its bruising like a grudge,

parroting *No one talks to me like that*
with a hard man look of malevolence.
We knew the fist couldn't be contained,
cooped up like a beast. Once the gloves were off

the fist shot out, seized its chance with both hands.
I backed off when the fist crashed through the door.
We hadn't hit it off too well: I'd keep
my head down if the fist was out for blood.

The onslaught caught the meeting on the hop.
The party chairman took it on the chin
when the fist attacked, driving home its point,
hitting the others where it really hurt.

It pointed the finger. A show of force
is needed, the fist declared, we must take
a firm grip before things get out of hand:
the fist came down in favour of hand-arms,

hand-guns, strongarm rule, the hands-on approach.
The fist banged the table. The fist was right.
The fist demanded a quick show of hands.
The meeting agreed to support the fist.

Led by the fist, the party faithful could
meet force with force, thrash the opposition,
beat up their candidates. Others the fist
discouraged from standing: their kneecaps smashed,

a smack in the jaw, some teeth to spit out,
a tongue stopped wagging in a handkerchief.
The fist worked hard on their image, made sure
their eyes had it, they'd no looks to speak of.

It rubbed them out, finished off their faces
like an artist; their likeness layered, furrowed
with palette knife, they almost looked alive.
The fist would drive them home, drop them off

at the front door, a present for the wife.
Some it slumped in a ditch, pushed from a car,
rolled from a bridge to float in public view.
Some it snatched in the high street as we looked

the other way, or ducked indoors, or froze.
No one raised a finger, or fought the fist's
election on a law and order vote.
The fist dismissed our Deputies, dissolved

the Senate and Supreme Court, established
its Provisional Government. It appeared
on TV in a general's uniform,
gauntleted on posters, on the new flag

the $50 note and ten cent stamp.
The fist regretted taking Special Powers,
needed the curfew kept from dusk to dawn.
The fist imposed internment, martial law,

a State of Emergency, with the troops
on red alert, the country on a war
footing, subversives and reds rounded up
for questioning, execution without trial.

The fist took a wife from the barrio,
wanting a son, a hundred years of rule
by fist and family. Each month's curse earned her
a beating on the bedpost, a fistfuck

for failure, exposure on the platform
at the march past. We all adored her like
a living saint, our Handmaid of the Fist,
our Black-Eyed Susan; after the fist broke

her cheekbone, we said Mass for her cracked jaw,
lit her candles, kept vigil till she died,
our Santa Susanna of the Head Wound.
When the U.S. froze its funds to the fist,

alleging it supported drug cartels
whose rake-off paid the army, the fist burned
their embassy, expelled the CIA,
blamed them for the national debt, secret deals,

conspiring with insurgents in the north.
The fist denounced its neighbours, sent conscripts
to the Border War, praised our purity
and pride as crops were rotting in the fields,

whole districts dying from the cholera.
The military refused to clear the square,
to waste the mothers of the disappeared.
We said the fist had lost its head, it slept

with a gun, a suitcase stuffed with dollars,
private jet on standby. It watched its guards,
the radar beeping like a heart, waiting
for the missed beat, the cardiac arrest.

Biting His Hand

He wanted me to take over the reins,
his inheritance safe with his daughter.
I certainly gave him that impression

when he was dying, and gave the order
that I should take his place. And now they come
asking me to give the usual favours.

I'm careful whom I help, biding my time
until I know I have enough support.
I test the water before each reform

I introduce, citing the argument
of economic need. The people grow
in their demands, and are more confident

the more I take their side, while seeming to
support the old régime. I've played along
with the army now for a year or two,

gaining their trust, their loyalty keeping
me at the helm. I have their acceptance
we cannot improve our trade and standing

unless we give the world the appearance
of democracy. The old guard agreed
to the army's request for elections,

thinking we were still putting up this front
to bring more money in. I think we now
have the right conditions. The rightists don't

like changes. They're plotting to overthrow
the government before the elections,
with me in charge as figurehead to show

my father's back in spirit, a return
to firm rule. I encourage them in this,
agree we've made too many concessions

to the left, foreigners and communists.
It's so like second nature, I almost
enjoy my back-to-basics rant, that this

country needs family values, and no votes
for anyone who can't write their own name.
They sing my name, give me the old blood toast,

take me into their confidence. My name
is still on their lips when they stage their coup,
calling the army to move in my name.

When the TV station's stormed in my name
the rightists hear me sing another tune.
I wear my army camouflage, my name

announced with a trumpet fanfare, my name
ordering the army back to barracks,
ordering them to back down in the name

of the people, the power of my name
splitting the army, loyal officers
arresting rebel generals in my name,

all the troops coming over in my name
to the loyalists in my father's name,
his martial son's who died in his name,

his daughter's to whom he gave his name
when she was christened, when she bit his hand,
when he joked she bit like him. In her name.

For Want of a Nail

Their leaders bought blind, because of the cost;
the MiG 15s (ex-Afghan) wouldn't fly.
The ground troops halted, the battle was lost,
the breakaway republic doomed to die
for want of support, *for want of a nail.*

The warring factions kept up their attacks
on the besieged enclave. Their envoy's news
didn't reach them, something wrong with the fax
from the Geneva talks. Their Christmas truce
shot down, the town fell, *for want of a nail.*

The radio went off the air, the rebels
stormed the presidential palace, but the
federal forces basted them, in Goebbels'
phrase, because they needed guns not butter,
for greasing the wheels, *for want of a nail.*

The surgeon needed sleep: the drip-feed's seal
was faulty, someone left a swab inside.
The new heart failed, the rupture wouldn't heal.
They kept him on dialysis: he died
for want of a bed, *for want of a nail.*

The cargo shifted, the bow doors weren't closed.
The lorry hit a car and shed its load.
She'd be here if the council hadn't closed
the school, she had to cross the busy road,
victim of the cuts, *for want of a nail.*

The walkway fell fifty feet from the deck.
Rescuers were late, the ambulance stalled.
The owners said there'd been a safety check
last year, it wasn't the company's fault
that corners were cut, *for want of a nail.*

warnings not heeded, *for want of a nail,*
nor safeguards observed, *for want of a nail,*
usual precautions, *for want of a nail,*
normal procedures, *for want of a nail,*
no proper funding, *for want of a nail.*

The phone line broke, the deadline expired,
they stormed the plane, the hostages were shot.
The talks broke down, the army marksman fired.
They couldn't reach the trapped people, and not
for want of trying, *for want of a nail,*

disaster waited, *for want of a nail,*
the president killed, *for want of a nail,*
his aides couldn't help, *for want of a nail,*
the government fell, *for want of a nail,*
a spokesman claimed, *for want of a nail.*

The Robber's Tale

The nail drove home. He saw it was well-oiled.
It hit something. It skidded in the wood.
The head whipped back on impact, and buckled.
He clawed the nail out. He did what he could.

The nail drove home. Jesus Christ did it hurt.
Then they ran out of tacks, but never fail,
the Romans had enough. So Christ died at
three, not two, and not for want of a nail.

Barabbas drove home. He had an hour's
start on Christ, whose car it was, his Vauxhall
Calvary, part of the deal: *My life for yours.*
Renew the disc. The tax ran out last fall.

He hit a checkpoint on interstate 10
south of Tyre, Roman paramilitaries:
This your car, sir? They nailed Barabbas then.
He was well-oiled: *Just breathe into this, please,*

render unto Caesar what is Caesar's.
He gave Tiberius a lung's breath of ale.
His head made headlines, falling down the stairs:
ROMANS QUIZZED OVER ROBBER'S DEATH IN JAIL.

John the Baptist at Ephesus

The temple arches to contain her light.
Her robes billow at the whispering windows.

Hidden from view, I shy from bare-breasted
priestesses with their cunt-scent offerings,

a truffle fisting beneath their dusty soles,
waiting for a pink snout to divine me

deep underground. When I feel a hound's teeth
gouge my grey flesh, I'll give up my god's head

like Orpheus, singing for the goddess
from a platter garnished with the sweetbreads

of prophetic loins, my green hair mottled
brown like the seeding broccoli that Paul

of Tarsus will describe in gourmet terms
in his fourth epistle to the Ephesians.

Make way for the head of broccoli!
Repent before the main course comes

in a creamy sauce. My spears will mushroom
with joy and butter in Diana's mouth.

The goddess will have me for breakfast
or my name's not St John of Brassica.

The Bollocks of King Henry VIII

Hurling or herding? For hurting more like:
our clanmen whirled these buggers widdershins
at Culloden, wooden curliewurlies
with pointy studs the English saw as stars.

Ma swung round: *you ould bollock-brain, you know*
they're Welsh, our Granda brought the bastards back
from Patagonia, his gaucho's bolas.
I know otherwise. They rattle like dags

from my rump. At night they hear me coming,
the other animals: Aberdeen Angus
with his clacking knackers of brown-stained oak.
I'm double-dandied with a shagdog tale

between my legs, a satyr after S
& M with a Welsh Blackface. Let's shoogie
to the Top Field, all you beasts. These beauties
are my chained curmudgeons, my best maracas.

Paul Hill Is Doing Bird

Paul Hill is doing bird in my cupboard,
an oil-slicked cormorant with lanky hair
he flicks from twitching eyes. He flaps about
like a sooty crow trapped in the chimney,

scuttling behind the wall. I tape his beak
to gag his squawking litany of jails:
Brixton to Parkhurst, Hull to Albany,
Wandsworth to Strangeways, Long Lartin, The Scrubs.

Moved without warning, from cupboard to chest,
from desk drawer to wardrobe, he won't escape
if he's cut off. He never sees the post
I send back marked *not known at this address.*

He's naked, a Sellotape body belt
holding him fast inside his jiffy bag.
When I don't starve him, he eats his breakfast
in the bag, before emptying his slops.

Dinner at twelve, slop out, then exercise,
an hour around the room; back to the bag,
tea at five, slop out, then six-thirty bed
unless my mates want to kick him about.

After fourteen years we enjoy our fun
with Paul Hill. An innocent jailbird can't
be reformed: he needs punishing instead
with a headbutt or punch in the groin.

We'd bugger him if he was bigger but
his bumhole's birdsize, I can't even get
a finger in, let alone a prick or fist.
To make him cough a dampened bag is best,

it sometimes gives him pleurisy. That way
he'll die inside, or if he's ever freed
he won't remember. I squash his appeal
from the jiffy bag. Watch the birdie bleed.

The Trojan War

Set in motion, the golden apple rolls
across the front line, targets beauty-
struck Paris. A weak man chooses wrongly.

Flash of fire: owl's eyes in the olive tree.
She feels his look, the pressure of his hand.
He steals a kiss. Now we're all at sea.

A raindrop breaks the ocean's back. On land
a butterfly beats its wings into a storm
a thousand miles away, our hopes sunk in this.

Shameless: wine-spotted sheets, his body on
her tongue, round wafer moon like honesty.
Beware the wooden horse of armistice,

belly bleeding. Men crawl out like insects.
Our gates open, forced to admit their will.
Chaos then. Their quick lust, our slavery.

Sea sucks at the hull, full moon pulls the tide.
My nipples quicken though my prince is dead,
a queen wet-nursing wolves. This way lies Rome.

Bird Woman

I fell asleep where a woodpecker drummed
his bill in a yew tree hollow, I felt
my refuge shudder, trembling like a man

at each axe blow, a beaten drumskin's cry.
I saw a wild buck mingle with the herd:
he turned tame, took food from my hand,

sired sturdy calves his same chestnut brown.
I placed his grey horns on my mother's grave
to let her talk with all the other dead.

Our trade with hairless men has brought disease.
The pasture's poor, the mothers limp, their young
are born two-headed or with swollen limbs.

The dead don't want us yet: we must move east
from the forest, ten days to good water.
My mother says avoid all woodcutters,

they turn to demons' dogs at dusk. I will
elude these wolvish men whose souls are loose,
I'll give their starling clouds the slip. When nights

are bad they shelter under docken leaves,
by yellow ragwort stalks, but I can soar,
I'm falcon now, or heron up aloft

watching my beasts, my body by the yew.
No devil's snake shall harm me there below,
no blind worms take me into darkest earth.

The keepers' boxes will not hold me long,
they stroke to life a bird with human head.
I will escape the great cold of the night.

Jehanne la Pucelle

It always started in the oakwood, as
the faintest riffle in the high branches.
I was a girl then, many times I felt it
but kept it to myself, a secret friend.
Like a blind woman I sensed their presence;
wanted to be held; cried to go with them.

I stopped bleeding when I went to the wood.
My mother worried. All the village cocks
had crowed the hour of my birth, the mark
on my breast showed an angel touched me there.
At Les Tourelles an English bowman pierced
that blessèd strawberry bruise. It healed itself.

When I refused to be betrothed, my brothers
would have drowned me. I fled to the oakwood
where the river dazzled, its crystal light
dancing like white fire, as sun and trees made
a Lorraine cross high in the canopy.
That sword shape I called Michel, for my country.

The whiteness was Catherine, like my sister,
who died a maid; Margaret, a mother's warmth
spreading through me. I called them voices but
I never heard them speak. I knew their word
through brilliance brighter than a thousand suns,
softer than ermine. And wept when they'd gone.

At Chinon, when I recognised the Dauphin,
I knew my Valois king as a woman
knows her own child, but spoke out as a man,
God's instrument. Riding my horse astride,
armoured as a knight, I took Orléans,
entered Rheims with Charles trotting at my side.

He doesn't need me now. My capture suits
the lot of them: the King; the Church; the Court.
The judge wants physical accounts of saints
I've never seen. I tell him lies to make
them believe, how I kissed an angel's feet.
My answers burn me. The truth is at stake.

The Rock Child

'All day I watched him from my hiding place,
a small child halfway down a rock platform
jutting out into the sea. I wanted
a closer look, but couldn't show myself

for fear I'd be picked up and taken back.
Silhouetted divers lined the ledge above
like spectral birds, their shadows mirrored in
the water. I half-hoped one might dolphin

from the sea to claim and carry off
the boy, but nobody came near; swimmers
went bobbing past like heads of Orpheus
echoing their cries. In the heat he seemed

to quiver, his mouth shaped as if to call,
but I was so far gone that day I'd not
have heard a scream. Sometimes I registered
a slight wave of the hand, but no one else

seemed to see him sitting there, not even
other children playing near. Yet he stayed
till the sun bled into dusk, when I know
I felt him keening like a wounded seal.'

'You sure it wasn't some trick of the light,
a rock shaped like a child?' 'A rock that moved?'
'The rock of Kounopetra used to rise
with the tide...' 'That child went into himself:

nobody looked for him, or checked his room;
he wasn't even missed at dinnertime.
When I crept back that night I had become
a ghost my family didn't want to see.'

The Magdalen Home Laundry

(West of Ireland, 1962)

I was shocked that first day I went to work
as a cook in the convent. As a child
I'd played by its high walls in the big field.
It gave me the creeps even then, that smoke

from its chimney like a crematorium.
The nuns would chase us if we came too close,
to stop us seeing, flapping like scarecrows.
I never knew what happened in the Home

until I took that job in the kitchens.
Every door you went through you'd to lock
behind you till you reached the laundry block.
They called them Marys, or the Magdalens:

sixty women crammed into one long room
lined with sinks, slaving over clergy clothes
at washboards, scrubbing at cassocks and cloaks,
wringing out that washing for a lifetime.

With red hands they scoured the stains of others,
girls with no knowledge of their own bodies,
betrayed by their own innocence. Families
handed them over; some of their mothers

threw them out when boyfriends refused to do
the right thing. They gave them to the nuns' care.
I saw slower girls dragged off by the hair
when they fell behind, and heaven help you

if you cried or gave the least back-answer:
you were the worst of outcasts then, not fit
to serve the Mercy Order; so they cut
your hair off, stopped your week's bag of sugar.

Those girls survived on bread and margarine.
They'd risk their Christmas soap and half a crown
to raid the bucket by the back kitchen
for scraps, when I'd pretend I hadn't seen.

Odd times I snatched words with them, when no one
was around; watched them gulp the tea I brought,
bolting back a biscuit. Scared they'd be caught,
their frightened faces looked out for the nun;

their bodies shook, even old Brid who'd been
a Mary since the days of the Free State.
Her sin was losing her way, being late
back from a dance, and she hadn't even

kissed the boy: forty years in the Home for
not being home by eleven o'clock,
as bad as the whores on Liverpool dock,
her Da said. When Brid asked what was a whore

in all innocence, the brute slapped her face.
She always had a trapped look in her eyes
but welcomed death, in the end, as release,
sure they'd judge her rightly in the next place

because they'd judged her wrongly here. I broke
the rules, took a glass of water to her
in the dormitory. Brid wanted a prayer,
an act of contrition, but when I spoke

I said her whole life was that, and I vowed
to help the other women, which I did.
Those I shut in the laundry hamper hid
in my god-fearing father's barn. A crowd

of guards came searching, but not one looked for
the loft, the obvious place. Those simple men
gave us faith, showed it was possible then
to be good by not seeing what they saw.

I Am Not Joanne Hayes

*'My life has become public property and my body a subject
for discussion all over the world'* – JOANNE HAYES, *My Story*

Abbeydorney

Evasion was an obsession with me.
I knew it was wrong, him a married man,
but put that from my mind. I didn't want
to think beyond the deep and total love

I felt for Jeremiah. When we made love
that time by the road in his car, I was
ready for him. I didn't ask had he a condom
others used for sex, not for love like ours.

For mine more like: I wanted nothing there
between us. When Yvonne was born, he broke
my heart, not leaving his wife, not wanting
to see his child. Yet I kept seeing him.

I wore loose clothes but thought the whole world knew.
Like later, everyone was watching me.
I ran away from them, pretended it
would disappear, nothing happen if I did

nothing. The night it came I felt hot
and feverish, but didn't think it was due.
I hadn't got as far as dates of birth.
It was the warm kitchen, the start of 'flu.

I felt nothing, went outside for some air,
there couldn't be a labour without pain.
I stood numbed, something thumped my stomach,
my waters burst. I stood alone in the field.

This isn't happening. No one knows I'm here.
I pull its head. *Mary Mother of God,*
it's on the grass. The cord inside me still,
my hands break it, my mind's blank. I'm not here.

There was no pain. Was that the afterbirth?
Kathleen calls from the house, am I all right?
My voice tells her a minute I'll be in.
I leave it lying there. I'm dreaming this.

This isn't me. I know it can't be there.
It didn't make a sound. I find myself inside,
taking off my dressing gown, wet with blood,
my nightdress bloody too. I run the tap

but don't hear water gush, my mind has gone
across the fields. Someone else's hands are
washing me, automatically. I press
a nightdress to my face, it smells of rain.

I lie in bed. It will not go away
even if I sleep. Wind blows round the house.
My sister Kathleen snores, oblivious.
I am alone. I'm scared to go outside.

I want to go but can't, I am afraid
of finding it alive, it would have been
my second. I didn't mean to harm it,
I couldn't hurt a child, not one of mine,

I've one of my own already. I love
Yvonne, pray God this one was dead or died
before it breathed, I didn't hear it make
a sound, it must have been, it wasn't time.

It's five o'clock. Bridie's in the kitchen.
I go down in my nightdress, drink some tea.
Outside I find the baby, pick it up,
don't look at it. I cover it with hay.

Go back to bed. Half-past-seven, get up.
I put the baby in a paper bag
inside a plastic bag, climb the bedstead
blocking the ditch, walk round the lower field

to find a hiding place, a water pool.
I left it there. And walked, not looking back.
I told them later in the hospital
I'd had a miscarriage. I had a shock

reading about the other child they found
at Caherciveen. It wasn't mine.
The Garda say they must be twins I had
by different men. Who do they think I am?

Caherciveen

I killed my baby. The family had gone
to Limerick for the day. When they came back
drunk with their luck, I'd had it on my own.
The wean had died. I put it in a sack.

They asked no questions. I said nothing more.
'We didn't need another mouth, that's sure,'
Da said, 'you did well there.' My brother Roy
was kinder, gave me £20 he'd won 'to buy

yerself a frock'. Ma said she didn't mind,
she knew I hadn't wanted it, the lad
had scooted off to England when he heard.
Me Da said his oul lot were always bad,

he'd thrash 'the daylights out of the wee shite'.
I tried to stop the brat. It wouldn't quit
bawling its head off, so I hit it like
me Da would when he got home, I hit it

with the laundry stick. When your Garda man
said Joanne Hayes had used 'a bathroom brush'
to hit the kid, I laughed at that, a bogbrush.
They got the knife wrong too. They said Joanne

had stabbed him in her room, she'd made a mess
with a carving knife from the kitchen drawer.
I wasn't doing all that in the house.
I went to the barn, did it on the floor.

I swept up afterwards and burned the straw.
The knife was Da's. The Garda man was sure
the child was killed by 'someone in a state
of frenzy', from all the wounds, twenty-eight

in the chest, four in the heart. But I must
admit I wasn't counting them, I just
wanted it to finish, I wasn't mad
or panicky. Next day me Da said where had

I put that oul bag?... didn't want no one
nosing round, knew it was fine, the poor wean
had been too weak, but he didn't need no
dealings with the Tralee Garda, he knew

what they was like, always grubbing for things
to pin on him. I showed him the Gouldings
0-7-30 fertiliser sack
the TV talked of, it weren't no turf sack

or manure bag the brothers Hayes were meant
to have used. We drove to White Strand, they went
to Slea Head, the other side of the bay.
The sack was washed up on the Saturday,

the gardai said the kid was dead four days
which means it must be mine, not Joanne Hayes'.
Our family liked the way she took the blame,
she was like one of us, a household name.

Ballad

There were three babies lay in a field,
  Down a downe, hay downe, hay downe,
There were three babies, one born in a field,
  With a downe,
There were three babies, one was killed,
Two were dead as they might be,
  With a downe Kerry, they were downe Kerry, downe.

One baby died in its mother's womb,
One baby died in her own bedroom.

One baby lived for a single day,
One baby lived a year and a day.

Joanne and Jerry were blood group O,
The baby in the pool the same group, so

the baby on the shore (blood group A)
was only hers as the Garda say

if she had twins by different men,
or one was hers, the other was mine.

Did hers live or did she let it die?
Did I make mine up or make it die?

Did our babies live and die the same?
I look like her. I have her name.

Our babies died in nineteen eighty-four.
Hers born then, mine the year before.

We saw her face on TV every day,
my face, my Joanne's face, made people say

'Aren't you that Joanne Hayes? I hope you win.'
They meant well. They couldn't know my pain.

They shouted 'Good luck Joanne' after me
as I fled from them, down Ormond Quay.

We ran away, left Dublin behind.
I left those who hurt me, being kind.

The Dressing Station

That last Easter, we read Wilfred Owen
in English, History reached 1916.
They rammed the Rising down our throats
as Thatcher's task force gave 'a bloody nose'

to Argentina. Going back to school
after the break, Anne Sheehan played the fool
and flirted with the young guard on the train.
He gave us the old joke: 'Limerick Junction,

change here for Galway and America.'
Anne said 'Let me go with you, Rebecca'
in the play interval. She was backstage
giving me my wounds, circling a bandage

around my turbaned hair, for my male part
in the phoney war we were acting out.
Proud of the Red Cross on her head, my nurse
fastened my dressings tight with safety pins,

giggling when Sister called my crutch a *crotch*.
As Anne leant over me, her strapless watch
bobbed on her breast, the buttons strained to burst
from the starched blue uniform. I blushed

as she talked of going over the top
with me in France. After we'd all packed up,
we tuned our secret radio upstairs
to BBC News on the World Service

and heard a Falklands sheepman's crackly voice
attacking 'the Occupation Forces'
in Port Stanley. I forgot the lock on
the prop cupboard and got a dressing down

next morning. Gunmen could have broken in
and stolen all our weapons, said the nun.
Those hunger strikers were desperate fellows.
The H-Block men would kill for arms like ours.

'The Desire To Be a Man'

(from Villiers de l'Isle-Adam)

You find yourself in France, outside a bar
in the Rue Hauteville. Its long mirror shows
the actor Esprit Chaudval, born Lepeinteur,
called Monanteuil, his many selves. He grows

old before our eyes, freed from parts of men
without grey hair. Your new role takes ten years
off your age. Chaudval says he hasn't been
a man, he's never known a love like yours

in all of France. You hadn't lived before.
So end this play-acting the loves and griefs
of others: Chaudval wants to feel the fear
of being wanted for murder, the deaths

of a hundred people on his conscience.
He fires an oil warehouse, the people die,
his act 'gratuitous'. Chaudval escapes
to his lighthouse, to feel the luxury

of his remorse, 'guarded from suspicion
by the grandeur of the crime'. No one knows,
no vengeful ghosts appear to torture him,
the sleepless nights he savours come because

he feels '*nothing – but absolutely nothing!*'
You felt nothing once. Now you burn because
you had her trust, you broke a heart, and nothing
hurt like that betrayal, her tears were yours.

You caused that conflagration. Like Chaudval
you fed it with your lies, and stood apart,
watching the flames go wild, out of control.
He wanted to 'see *true* ghosts', but his heart

was never in it: your ghosts roast yours on
a real-life spit in your own Gothic romance.
He 'owed himself to himself', a fiction
you made happen, leaving her to live in France.

Night Work

You are the envy of your colleagues here
working under someone they call charming.
He's nervous, gesturing to touch your hair
on the way out. He finds you disarming,

having to compliment your work, the kind
of praise you like. But then you see that's why
he gives that line. The others say you'd find
it easier to play along. Your way

is harder when you know he likes it more,
your game of cat and mouse. You mean it when
you turn down a dinner at the *Coq d'or.*
He persists: 'Why this working late again?'

You smile at his advice: 'You should go home.'
'I have my work': you flatter to deceive,
preparing for next week's trip to Rome,
on his business, you've led him to believe.

The last girl slept with him. It's in the file
they showed you when you said: 'You want his ass,
I'll get it but I won't give you a thrill.
I'll want to keep intact my alias.'

You screw him your way, spend the night inside
his computer. Using his key, you let
yourself into his system. Passwords hide
a labyrinth of files. The syndicate

is somewhere there, but nothing's obvious.
There is no missing entry or mistake.
You look for something wrong or out of place.
It has the flawless beauty of a fake

when you spot it: two matching quota stats,
a double claim for Italy and Spain,
two payouts, one receipt, two duplicates.
It proves he isn't working on his own,

there's too much at stake. It makes you shiver,
you look behind you as the print-out whirs
from the machine. You're scared but still admire
his cleverness, the clean way he covers

his tracks, unrevealing like his uncreased
Armani suit, his always tidy desk
at which you sit, uneasy as a priest,
unused to sins you copy on your disk.

You're edgy in the métro, change trains twice,
switch to a cab, looking round all the time
for the right night-safe. Someone else will trace
his funds to arms or international crime.

They'll keep him on to keep the link alive.
You'll watch him while you put him at his ease,
but put him off your scent. He must believe
no one knows, he's in control. If he sees

you think he's watching you with anything
other than preying eyes, they'll close him down.
You'll want him interested, keep him dangling
but at the right distance, on a taut line.

You don't want them to pull you out before
your work's done. You want to leave with a smile,
him not knowing whom he has to thank for
his arrest after a safe interval.

You ponder facts, your power over lives.
You know enough to put a man inside,
holding his fate in your disk, and his wife's,
his public disgrace, perhaps her suicide.

Biting My Tongue

I push away my spoon, remember not
to blow the soup, rather have it burn
my tongue than let them see I haven't grasped

their habits of a lifetime. I had to learn
to eat with their ease, small talk in the tongue
our mother sang, lulling us children

asleep. I am a caged bird mimicking
her singing voice, suppressing my mother
tongue to think in hers, never struggling

as my father did when she trapped him here
with relatives, a beast they wanted back
with his own kind. My mother watched him paw

exotic carpets, angered by their lack
of understanding; later gave me codes
I'm using, even down to how I knock

my glass over, to go and change my clothes
while they're downstairs. I have time to try out
the next piece of body language I'll use

returning to the group, something they taught
in movement at the house, that I practised
in the mirror. They had a word for it

I can't recall, the studied natural twist
my hands and body give this *quatorze* chair
as a mumbling dinner guest swoops and lifts

his ushering arms. I use their murmur
of welcome back to introduce my switch
in speech to second person familiar,

engaging my host's attention in such
a way as signals he might speak with me
afterwards, at his initiative, which

I need for my plan. Now I'm free to be
more personal, I add authentic spice
to their banter. Each gives their recipe

for removing wine. My mother's advice
becomes my own. I have to bite my tongue
to tell it, needing to apologise

for its coarser elements, but knowing
this shrug of mine confirms my native wit.
I set their tongues wagging when I'm on song.

Double Act

The devil's done your work: the powder's mixed,
the white salt pure. Fix yourself your cocktail
for tonight: just add two drops of tincture,
melt the crystals, make the compound red.

You watch it fuming in your measured phial,
bubbling like your blood, hissing to the boil,
then swelling to a purple fizzing head,
to green like *crème de menthe*. You've never felt

a thirst, a pull as strong, it's reached the point
of no return. You grab the glass, and gulp
the liquid back as greedily as when
you press your lips around your lover's cunt.

You hold her picture, almost smell her skin,
you see her red-brown hair, her sassy eyes;
you stroke her back, freckled like a thrush's breast,
her waking nipples playing with your tongue,

her hungry belly where you lose your head.
You waltz your feel of her around the room,
putting on your top hat, white tie and tails.
The cheval-glass shows you someone else

touching your shirt with unfamiliar hands.
They brush down your dress suit, display your nails
like jewellery. The mirror shows you taller,
a dark stranger holding yourself with ease,

devil-may-care charm in that reckless way
you wear your hat, the way you hold your cane,
they can't take that away from you. You cough
nervously, discovering a new voice

you'll have to practise on your own, know how
to change back to the good doctor's, put on
the mask of his respectability,
the man who's married to your gentle wife.

You sleep with her. You're putting on his clothes.
You use his quiet tone to ask the maid
to press your tie, but whose tongue lashed out
when she burned your meal? Or was it his?

You meet the butler on the stairs, who says
good evening to a man he thinks he knows
as master of his house. You're stepping out,
my dear, to breathe an atmosphere that simply

reeks with class: there may be trouble ahead,
but while there's moonlight and love and romance,
you'll walk on air, you'll hoof it down the street,
tapdance down the Old Town's darkest wynds,

you'll hop along the cobbled close, flip round
to face the music, fell the chorus gents
parading disapproval on the Mile
with a rat-tat-tap on your shooting-stick.

You've had her invitation in the mail.
Your presence is requested at her side.
You're wearing your top hat, white tie and tails.
You're out together dancing cheek to cheek.

You draw her with your outlaw style, pull her
towards you, feel her waver, suspicious
as a chorus girl, snaking like a cat.
Give her your balletic turn, then come out

with some ballroom moves, a jazz kick and slide.
You tap, she taps, you smile, you're close again.
Circling the floor, arm in arm, you match
each other, step for step, in perfect time.

And pause. You take her hands in yours, and gaze
into those green-brown eyes. You hesitate on
the brink of something you both want but fear.
Camera comes in close, holding your mouths caught

wanting to kiss, a recognition in
her eyes, the way they're burning into yours,
acknowledging to you alone she's stirred
beneath her sequinned dress, as you are pressed

against her thigh, not hiding this from her.
Now go footloose, do the Carioca,
your new rhythm, your blue rhythm that sighs.
Then do the Continental, switch to end

on the Piccalino, whisking her round
in faster circles, till you lift her up
as the music mounts, the big band rises
to its final brassy note, your hands round

her thighs, your smile directed at the V
her scissor legs display above your mouth.
Your arms ache, hold her balanced in the air,
ease her down, slowly, bring her back to you.

She falls back as the credits roll, herself
as Ginger Rogers, you playing yourself,
the dancer and good doctor in real life,
another double she will recognise,

all characters completely fictitious
except the author, any resemblance
to living or dead a coincidence
(apologies to Fred and RLS).

All rights reserved. Song lyrics by Gershwin
and Berlin. Ensembles by Hermès Pan.
Mandy at Sherlock for Miss Rogers' hair.
© Rebecca Hayes, 1994.

Biting Her Tongue

How could she let her know? She longed to lie
(she knew she had repressed it for too long).
She'd tell her, but she'd never have her cry.

Her love was a betrayal, and to try
to hide it a deception just as wrong.
How could she let her know? She longed to lie,

say nothing and they needn't say goodbye.
Her love had been presumption all along:
she'd tell her but she'd never have her cry!

She knew it was impossible so why
this hopeless exercise, this two-tongued song?
How could she let her know she longed to lie

touching her skin, and kiss her breasts, her thigh?
She'd never sleep beside her all night long.
She'd tell her, but she'd never have her cry

she wanted her, nor ever hear her sigh.
She had to say the whole idea was wrong:
how could she let her know? She longed to lie.
She'd tell her, but she'd never hear her cry.

Electricity

They're dangerously close, live and neutral
almost touching, the red coded L

is charged, the blue called N for negative
resistance excited with the pull of LIVE.

Between them space becomes electric,
a force field drawing like to unlike,

a hair's breadth quickening of breath.
Red is glowing, smouldering as if

on fire, slowly tensing to the point
of magnetism. Blue, attracted,

still holds back, then starts to melt, wavers
like a needle – its pulsing registers

the drag of gravity. Like lightning
darting across space, blue's tongue

spurts a dazzling rush of sparks:
a bolt of electricity zips

round all the house's hidden circuits,
slamming its foundations, shoots

out like a firework, a jazzy starburst
fizzing red with its *zzzzzt zzzzzt zzzzzt!*

And the wind goes wild with the house, hisses
disapproval of their tingling kisses,

as blue-white heat is earthed in red,
shocking the walls, rocking the bed.

'hey know you're huddled there
hearing something outside
ıck, some kind of cry. You want
to go ᴛᴏ ᴛ.. indow, drawn by a tree's
death-rattle *rat-tapping* on your pane.

Your heartbeat lurches with the wind, you can't
shut out the whispering of this Monday night,
its rustling voices: those who wanted you
and those you've loved or lost are merging with
the risen dead, a voice high as a wolf's

breathing your name through this night and the next.
You watch the ceiling's mottled shapes become
a face, the shadows playing on a mouth
enticing you outside, *come walk barefoot
in the cold grass*, your nightdress trailing wet.

Wednesday night you're at the window, the face
reflected out there, watching from a room
which mirrors yours, telling you to step out
into the rain and howling dark. You want
to reach across, to go to him. You have

to stop yourself. Thursday's wild, it has you
tossing with the storm, you're grappling to hold
that wraith, to feel whatever form he takes
against your naked body, to let him
enter you, come inside you like a god

become a snorting bull with horns of gold,
a swan with beating wings. Friday the face
has gone, you're left with a longing, an ache
of absence, feeling someone dead's about
to call you, someone travelling through the dark

who may not reach you for another night.
Midnight Saturday, you wait for the wind
to force the casement, fling it open as
it roars in tearing at the curtain gauze
flailing ghostly white like a bridal veil,

the dark figure bending to kiss your neck.
Sunday, the Lord's Night when you listen for
a hoof knock on the door, the heavy tail
he drags behind him, scratting claws you hear
before the great key grinding in the lock.

He drops his cloak into a shadow, kneels
beside your bed. Reaching to stroke his fur
your fingers touch the bristles on his skin;
you're shocked they prick your flesh, as you hold him
in your arms, with the dark night closing in.

That Kiss

That fleeting kiss we snatched when no one saw,
it caught us unawares: your eyes drew mine,
we joined that moment when the creature came
into our mouths, that kiss our fearful tongues
were wanting to enflesh, lingering there
on lips left thirsting for the beast itself.

I nurse it like a secret for that time,
a mother fish with young inside my mouth.
Its pursing urgent as an orphan lamb's,
I keep it warm and lick it into shape
for you, I let it play upon that thought
until it burns like whiskey on my lips.

The little devil's restless, mewling for
our mouths to melt in moist release. That kiss
is drawing us together, wanting you
to give me back the pressure of my lips;
your breath snuffling my skin (its tiny hairs),
prickling my breasts, my ticklish clitoris.

From a Previous Life

It was a cat jostling with its shadow
through the mist, pursued by a pool of darkness,
when it seemed to change, the shadow somehow
spilling away, like a sloughed coat, a stain
dissolving with the night through the wet grass.
An hour passed. With each circling of the house

it came closer, more like a dog, grey fur
glistening with an icy starburst of dew.
Then stood at the door like an accusation,
gazing at me inside. I watched its snout
press a fruit bruise on the cross-wired glass,
ghosting the window with a wraith of breath.

My eyes glazed over. I moved in a dream
towards the shivering creature, and knelt there,
teeth chattering, my whole body trembling as
with fear, or fever – something that felt more
like... was it love? Kneeling like St Francis,
or open-mouthed Teresa caught in prayer,

I froze into its wide-eyed stony stare,
wanting its wild hunger to strip me bare,
to peel away my bark, layer after layer.
Skinned to white marble, by this love, raw
like a saint's, a statue moved to the door,
a miracle, shedding a single tear.

A Single Tear

'The gigantic weight of a single tear' – SYLVIE GERMAIN

Running down my face, a single tear
these days apart, a salt trail between
countries, falling like cities in a war,

the gigantic weight of my tearing
heart, breaking from my eye
as we parted, still on my cheek

after weeks, *une larme*, a sense of alarm,
a grieving house wanting you back,
mirroring our love, dissolving ash,

quenching flame and thirst, a cure
for heartbreak, a tear drop
under a microscope, a droplet

holding breath, rivulet through dust,
river nothing evaporates, enters
the sea, rises in air to fall as

a raindrop swells, a gigantic tear
running down your face, enters
your mouth, my tear wanting to reach

your tongue, to taste inside
your mouth, my lips
tear into you

The North Country

You cry in sudden panic, an old pain
stabbing your back you thought you could escape.
The wound reopens like a punctured vein,
a nightmare vision, a memory of rape.

Your tears swell with shadows from the old house,
strangers appearing from the north like death.
You loved that place. They flayed you from its walls,
scoured out your spirit, choked the chimney's breath.

Despite the hurt, you let me draw you close.
I want to draw a new house from your wounds.
It holds you like a second skin, and grows
intimate with us, sharing all your moods.

You've come home here. Let us lay our scent down,
know it as closely as each other's skin,
warm to each inch, each freckled patch where sun
glows on cayenne walls, love it like children.

Homecoming

(from a line by Neruda)

'El cielo es una red cuajada de peces sombríos'

The sky's a net crammed with shadowy fish.
My boat heaves through dark water, a drunk whale
diving to dodge the shadow-spearing gulls
dashing themselves in its white foaming trail.

Urging the ship, I pace the deck, restless
as a pawing beast, snorting to be loose,
coaxed by arms of land beckoning the boat
into harbour. Hearing your siren voice,

I jabber strange cries like a crazed seabird,
drawn home on a wave of longing. I feel
like a fish writhing to release my sperm
upstream, sleeved inside you, wagging my tail.

Sweetheart Abbey

'At Sweetheart Abbey
sea-mist licks red stone, crisp frost:
you keep my breast warm.'

They really call it that. The tale warms us:
the good Lady Devorgilla buried
with her husband's embalmed heart. She'd kept it
in a casket till she gave up the ghost.
I take your picture, winter-coated in

an arch of sandstone, red walls softened by
a blur of mist. The deserted abbey's
open to the elements, its windows
wide-eyed like the look you give my camera
and those dogs, brazen in their play. This gift

of Sweetheart Abbey's irresistible:
our hearts' desire preserved not only in
your photograph – the way it makes my heart
leap into life each time I take it from
the box – but more in knowing we'll be joined

in what we'll give each other when we're home.
You read me yours from England on the phone.
In mine the heart has a life of its own,
grabs you from behind; and chilled to the bone,
we fuck like dogs on Sweetheart's holystone.

The Colour Bled

Where red begins, I see the colour bled.
I call it bled because it glows with blue
agate's translucency. I'm off my head.
I'm colour mad. I cry my hue for you.

I kept it quiet. No one else saw bled.
I knew the colour blind can't see or feel
under the surface. They think blood is red
but wounds are bled when fresh, before they'll heal.

The day I died the light I saw was bled.
I floated in a bled mist in the ward
above the men who thumped me on the bed.
A diamond roselight beckoned me upward,

the tunnel led to a cervix of bled.
There was more bled than a body can bear.
I wanted mine back. I reached down and said
to my whitecoat assailants: *hang on there,*

that's my body you're hitting there! It bled
and hurt, but felt like a dream. I was back!
My naked body bled with you in bed,
the lovely feel of me came eeling back,

your kissing made me come all over bled.
As I lay flying there, I said my book
would tell you all the properties of bled.
Everybody's forgotten how to look

for true colour, for the feeling of bled,
since bled's the colour of amnesia,
and death releases bled. Lost souls are bled,
old pain, new love and sexual pleasure.

When the moon is in Neptune I feel bled,
the bled planet colours how I think.
Songs played in B sharp sound as if they're bled.
I write this in the bleddest kind of ink.

White

'The mirror too is a window.
If I jump from it I will fall into my arms.'
    YANNIS RITSOS

White like an afterglow of snow, the room; white as cream
the stippled walls, its naked bulb-light. As the sun glares
from the whitewashed courtyard up through rood-screen trellises

of greening vine-trails, the window's tinted to stained glass.
Below a clock and wooden crucifix, the bed stripped,
an altar cloth of white linen. The mirror faces

a mirror opposite, window on another room
with bed and crucifix, then another white within,
another room beyond, each whiter than the other;

each crucifix is more contorted, figuring pain
thirteen times replayed. The white beds repeating themselves
make a glass-screened hospital, but from the distant door

no apparition comes; no Carmelite, her cornette
lappeted with starched white sails, tends a line of soldiers
white-bandaged from the front; no white-hooded votary

bobs like the harvest moon through the night clouds: only on
the furthest bed, bleeding from inside, like a woman,
a pale man scrats his nails on glass like chalk on blackboard.

His pallid skin's tracery is the face of the moon,
his constellation of scars spilling a milky stream
into a long white scratch pulsing red, shooting across

the glass to a crack in the mirror, through which the man,
naked, hauls himself, unhelped, from bed to blood-streaked bed,
hour by hour his progress tolled by clocks when each implodes.

As the next mirror shatters, again he breaks though glass
into another room with a white bed unbloodied
when he heaves himself up. As the last clock strikes thirteen

he finds himself in the last room, the first room now white
in the moonlight, where the crucifix uncarves itself
to a wooden block he makes his pillow. He lies down

on a white bed jewelled with glass, bedecked with uncoiled
clock springs, a pendulum rolling like a lost oar as
the bed, like the moon's white boat, moves with his slow breathing.

He sleeps unaware the bed is caulked as his blood flow
is staunched, but of this, the blood, he remembers nothing
waking then in the white room, warm with the afterglow

of last night's long loving with the white-towelled woman
whose mirrored eyes absorb his gaze, her circling fingers
creaming her face with lotion white as the morning sun.

My Demon Lovers

Coming on her asleep in a forest
clearing, stripped naked as a winter tree,
he quick-changed into goggling wolf, to feast

on breasts while gobbling her, tugged her free
of clinging tree limbs, not before she stopped
his jaws, flexing firm her boa'd body

to pike his throat, and then erupting, wrapped
his neck round, her coil of muscled snake
wring-pulling his swelling head, till he slipped

himself free, leaped rearwards to attack
her as a hellish civet, wiry-haired,
demon-eyed devouring her with a look

of pure devilment, speckly-pink gums bared
to eat her whole, his tongue low-lolling, forked
to divine her well, his pounce she countered

with her fastest switch, sloughing off a rucked
and concertina'd snake-sleeve to emerge
a Bengal tiger, mounted and fucked

him like damnation, their horny frottage
boned him, barking mad, rocked into tree
she clove him trunk to root, her hoofed discharge

of lightning shuddering him out of his tree,
quenching him headlong in river
plunge through Eden's azure which she,

the redhead sun, shot through with light of a
kindness he'd never known, crystal-raining
down, drinking each other's fire-water

torrenting, her tongues of flame delighting
his tensed skin, an insect water-skater
licking water-lily lips, extinguishing

their long burn in light-play on water,
misting together, his hot spring sprinkling
into gentle shower, they rolled over

their river-bed, heads and tails lunging
in and out, each chasing the other,
paws and hooves a-fly, sinning tongues singing

till they lay on the far side together,
rakehelly, no more damned changes to ring,
ram-wolf with civet cradled by tiger,

her jasper-yellow 'n' black stripes snaking
furred limbs around him, demon lover
addressing hell-mate in the slaking

tongue of our coke 'n' sulphur-sniffer
down El Diablo's way, in Belial's ling-ling:
That was trooly delish, one hell of a

fook, my black shepe, no need woolly's clothing
to fleece my fancie, you tasty geyser,
lingo'd the lewd tyger, as snout snuffling

he wolfed down her strawberry-velvet oyster:
Paradise, the catte quoth, wet-whiskering,
Let's out wi' a bang for ould Lucifer.